4X 12/01 LT 5/00
5X 6/03 7/03

D0742950

A Book about a Girl with MENTAL RETARDATION

Leslie's Story

Text and photographs by Martha McNey
with Arc of Hennepin County

⌐ LERNER PUBLICATIONS COMPANY / MINNEAPOLIS

LIBRARY OF CONGRESS CATALOGING-IN-PUBLICATION DATA

McNey, Martha.
    Leslie's story : a book about a girl with mental retardation/text and
photographs by Martha McNey with Arc of Hennepin County.
      p. cm.
    Summary: Describes the home and school life of twelve-year-old Leslie,
a girl with mental retardation, and discusses mental retardation in general.
    ISBN 0-8225-2576-3 (alk. paper)
    1. Mental retardation — Juvenile literature. 2. Meningitis —
Complications — Juvenile literature. [1. Mental retardation. 2. Mentally
handicapped.] I. Fish, Leslie. II. Title.
RJ506.M4M34   1996
362.3'092 — dc20
  [B]   95-35621

Manufactured in the United States of America
1 2 3 4 5 6 – JR – 01 00 99 98 97 96

Dedicated to Mary Jo Malach,
passionate advocate for people with disabilities

Author's Note

Leslie Fish is one of more than 7 million Americans who have mental retardation, and one of more than 43 million people in America who have disabilities.

The Americans with Disabilities Act of 1990 paved the way for people with disabilities to claim their place as equal citizens in the United States. The act made it illegal to discriminate against people with disabilities in the workplace, at school, and in other public places.

Now the biggest challenge is overcoming the kind of discrimination that can't be controlled by laws—discrimination in the ways people think about and treat those who have disabilities. Leslie and I hope this book will help all people with disabilities gain acceptance and respect.

CONTENTS

HI! MY NAME IS LESLIE FISH. I'm twelve years old. I live in Plymouth, Minnesota, a suburb of Minneapolis.

I'm a little different from most kids my age. When I was a baby, I had a disease called meningitis. It gives you a high fever. My parents had to race me to the hospital. You can die from meningitis, or go blind, or have to use a wheelchair. The disease damaged my brain. It gave me mental retardation, which means it takes me longer to learn things than other people. But I don't like the term "mental retardation." I say I'm handicapped.

My handicap makes it tough for me to pay attention, and
I need to wear hearing aids, because the meningitis made
me lose some of my hearing. I used to have seizures—I'd
black out and fall on the floor and my body would shake.
I was really scared. Now I take medicine to prevent seizures.

8

Once in a while I do things I can't help, like make sounds or talk to myself or act sort of babyish. But mostly, I'm just like everyone else. This book is about my life.

My mom's name is Rosemary. We both have freckles. My mom does a lot of volunteer work for disability organizations.

We like to do lots of things together, like reading,
shopping, and going to movies. We make pudding. Yum!

My dad's name is Marvin. He's a stockbroker. Sometimes
we pretend to smoke cigars, to be funny.

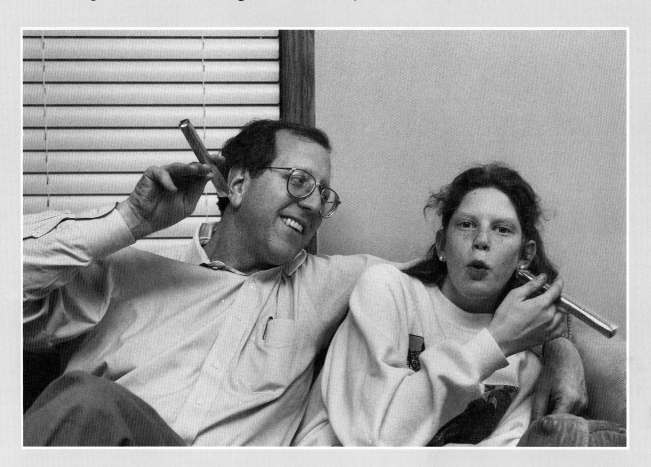

We like to play pool together. I'm almost winning!

Matt is my brother. He's 15. If people make fun of me, Matt explains to them why I'm different. Skiing is our favorite sport. Matt checks the bindings on my skis to make sure they're safe. Matt shows me how to tighten the bindings so my feet will stay in the skis.

Now we're ready to go skiing. We've skied many places in Minnesota and in Vail, Colorado.

I WAS IN SPECIAL EDUCATION CLASSES all day at school until fifth grade. Now I go to Plymouth Middle School and have classes with everyone else. Math class is first hour. My favorite class is physical education. I also go to speech therapy, because I have a hard time hearing some sounds and I need to work on speaking more clearly.

My friend Liz helps me in reading class. She also stands up for me and tells me not to pay attention if other kids say things that hurt my feelings. Sometimes kids are mean to me. They hit me or pull my hair. Boy, does that make me upset. But I don't cry until I get home. My mom calms me down and helps me feel better. She tells me I'm tough and that I should avoid mean people.

Some days after school I go to art class at a community art center. My favorite things to draw are shapes—circles, squares, triangles, diamonds, plus shapes I make up myself.

I think I did a good job on my drawing.

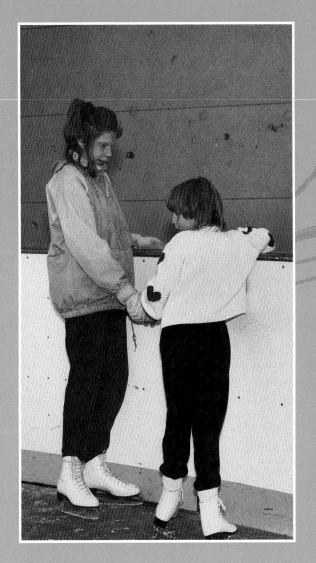

I ALSO TAKE ICE SKATING LESSONS. My teacher is Elaine. When other kids have trouble skating, I help them. I love to go fast on the ice. Where I live, it's cold outside a lot. It's easier to get through the winter if you like outdoor sports, such as ice skating.

One year I skated with my Special Olympics team at the National Figure Skating Championships. Special Olympics is a sports contest like the regular Olympics, but only people who have mental disabilities can take part.

People with disabilities aren't all the same. Not everyone can do the same things. Some people with disabilities like lifting weights or swimming. I like to skate. I've belonged to Special Olympics since I was eight. I love it.

My friend David takes skating lessons with me. He used
to live across the street from me. We've been friends since we
were five years old.

Sometimes after school I call my best friend, Aleeza. It's fun to talk to her on the phone.

It's even more fun when she comes over to my house. We do art projects, play basketball, and go Rollerblading.

CLOSE TO MY 13TH BIRTHDAY, I celebrate my Bat Mitzvah. It's a Jewish ceremony that means I'm an adult and I can help carry on the traditions of my religion. First I had to study Hebrew for five years. That was hard! I also wrote my own speech for the ceremony.

In my speech I talk about taking responsibility for myself, and about being brave enough to tell people when they do things that are wrong or bad. I'm proud of myself. My Bat Mitzvah makes me realize I can do almost anything if I try hard enough. When I get older I want to work as a helper for kids with physical handicaps.

Information about
MENTAL RETARDATION

Mental retardation means that a person has below average intelligence. People with mental retardation score lower on intelligence tests than other people, and they may have a harder time getting along in the world by themselves.

About three percent of the people in the United States have mental retardation. Some people are affected more than others. Some children's retardation may not be recognized until they go to school and have trouble learning.

There are many different causes of mental retardation. Not all of them are known. Mental retardation can be the result of disease or injury, or it may be present from birth. It might happen if a woman becomes sick while she is pregnant, or if she drinks too much alcohol. Some forms of retardation are caused by a genetic defect.

Most people with mental retardation live at home or in some kind of community home, where a group of people live, often with a counselor or someone else who helps them. Many children with mental retardation attend classes with other students. Adults with mental retardation often learn job skills and become good workers.

Many people with mental retardation, like Leslie, do not like to use the terms "mental retardation," "mentally retarded,"or "retarded." They might say they have a developmental disability, or a disability.

For more information about mental retardation,
you can write or call:

American Association on Mental Retardation
    444 Capitol Street NW, Suite 34
    Washington, DC 20001
    (202) 387-1968

Council for Exceptional Children
    1920 Association Drive
    Reston, VA 22091
    (703) 620-3660

The Arc: A National Organization on Mental Retardation
    500 East Border Street, Suite 300
    Arlington, TX 76010
    (800) 433-5255

Special Olympics, Inc.
    1325 G Street NW, Suite 500
    Washington, DC 20005
    (202) 628-3630

GLOSSARY

Bat Mitzvah—(BAHT mitz-vah) a Jewish ceremony that marks a girl's coming of age, signaling that she is an adult and can carry out religious responsibilities

developmental disability—a mental or physical disability that limits life activities. Developmental disabilities include mental retardation, cerebral palsy, autism, and visual impairment

disability—a limitation that interferes with a person's ability to function—for example, to walk, talk, hear, or learn

disabled—mentally or physically challenged or impaired

discrimination—(dis-CRIM-ih-NAY-shun) unfair treatment based on something such as race or disability

genetic—(juh-NET-ick) having to do with the information in the body that is passed on from one generation to the next

handicapped—*See* disabled. The terms disabled and handicapped mean the same thing, but different people may prefer one term or the other.

meningitis—(men-in-JYE-tus) a disease that affects the brain and spinal cord

mental retardation—a condition marked by below average intelligence and development

seizure—(SEE-zhur) involuntary muscle movement or brief loss of consciousness

Special Olympics—a sports competition for people with mental retardation and other disabilities

About the AUTHOR

Martha McNey spent three years as communications coordinator for Arc of Hennepin County, a nonprofit organization that serves people with developmental disabilities and their families. Currently she works as a communications specialist for an environmental engineering firm. She lives in Excelsior, Minnesota, with her husband and daughter.

Read about other children who successfully deal with special life circumstances in Lerner's *Meeting the Challenge* series.

Alison's Story: A Book about Homeschooling, with text and photographs by Jon Lurie.
Carolyn's Story: A Book about an Adopted Girl, with text and photographs by Perry Schwartz.
David's Story: A Book about Surgery, with text and photographs by Benjamin Brink.
Nicole's Story: A Book about a Girl with Juvenile Rheumatoid Arthritis, by Virginia Totorica Aldape, with photographs by Lillian S. Kossacoff.
Zack's Story: Growing up with Same-Sex Parents, by Keith Elliot Greenberg, with photographs by Carol Halebian.

Lerner Publications Company, 241 First Avenue North, Minneapolis, MN 55401, toll-free 800-328-4929.